FOOTPRINTS

Ioanna Tsatsos

Footprints

English version by Jean Demos

Hellenic College Press
Brookline, Massachusetts 02146

Published by Hellenic College Press
50 Goddard Avenue
Brookline, Massachusetts 02146

Cover design by Mary C. Vaporis

Library of Congress Cataloguing-in-Publication Data

Tsatsou, Ioanna.
[Ichnelasies. English]
Footprints/Ioanna Tsatsos: English version by Jean Demos.
p. cm.
Translation of: Ichnelasies.
ISBN 0-917653-31-9 (pbk.)
1. Tsatsou, Ioanna—Journeys—Israel. 2. Authors, Greek (Modern)—20th century—Journeys—Israel. 3. Israel— Description and travel—1981- I. Title
PA5631.S37I2413 1988
889'.83403—dc19
[B]
88-16420
CIP

Contents

A Call

You called me

Step by step
I climb the hard road
I want to reach You
My strength so little
My anxiety unstilled

You stand beside me
In the slippery snow
In the frost that cuts off my breath

You give me strength
In the smile of a child.

A few words

A Few Words

The path to Jesus is hard for me. I feel this with all my heart and mind. Like Peter, I step on angry waves, hoping to reach Him. But even more, I feel with burning heart that only He exists. And when my faith falters and I flounder, He comes to me and takes me by the hand:

O woman of little faith, why do you hesitate?

In this hope, I shall try to write these pages.

An unexpected invitation

An Unexpected Invitation

What was this unexpected invitation?[1]

Why did the light which had gone out suddenly shine again of itself?

We must not miss this journey.

Why, buried deep inside me, is there this unconquerable nostalgia for a land I do not know?

For years now, imagining that land has been as natural to me as breathing, and is that not a kind of knowledge?

We must not miss this journey.

Furthermore, I know that if I do miss it, all my life I shall be psychically crippled.

Nor does logic help me to cope with this torturing desire.

So I began my preparation. Day by day I concentrated on His thought and on the holy texts.

I was studying the Old Testament carefully as far as the most inspired chapters of the Prophecy. How otherwise could I hope to understand the land of the Gospel, the tradition, the environment of Jesus?

---

[1]The Jewish community of Thessalonike decided to found a Greek branch for classical studies at the University of Jerusalem in memory of the 65,000 Jewish students martyred in the Nazi concentration camps. They invited former President Constantine Tsatsos to inaugurate it.

How could I better understand the Law, the wisdom stamped with the presence of the One God and His righteousness?

Paul was to say to the Romans:

Christ is the end of the Law. (Romans 10.4)

The gate will be closed

The Gate Will be Closed

This sentence from Ezekiel expresses all the patience and hope of the Scriptures. The sufferings of history will be erased in time; the closed gate will open so that the eternal Christ may pass through.

The Bible begins with that perfect poetic word: creation.

In the beginning God created . . .
And the earth was without form and void, and darkness was upon the face of the deep . . . And God said, 'Let there be light' and there was light.
(Genesis 1.1-3)

And we meet this light, this poetry, at every step — in texts, in phrases, in cruel accounts of battle — a star in dark heavens. It is a living spring because it touches the very essence of life.

In solitude consciousness senses that "we know in part" and is then left free to listen for the mystery. God above the Logos is there. He will start the hymn. He will grant the gift of prophecy.

In the Bible, sometimes in many words, sometimes briefly, between the lines we hear vibrations beating out the rhythm of a hidden life. Thus God's secret is united with human longing. What we sense is an additional route to understanding.

Thus we learn that among the ruins and hopes throughout the ages the Great Expectation is summoning the Lord.

Throughout the Old Testament, God is one and only one. In the early centuries, in Exodus, Judges, Kings, in the Prophets, Yahweh is present at every step.

He is on the battlefield with the Chosen People. He founds the kingdom of Israel. It is something unique and marvelous that with such faith and perseverance, such vigor, this small primitive people dedicates itself utterly to its stern God. And most difficult of all, to the spiritual God who embodies what was then man's highest moral position:

I do not desire sacrifice,
but I desire righteousness
and respect for the weak —

So David would say in his Psalms.

*

*   *

The enduring marvel, the incredible miracle, is that of the Exodus and Moses. The only one who spoke with God Himself. The only one who heard His terrifying definition, the definition that plunged man into nothingness.

"I AM THAT I AM."

He led the twelve tribes of Israel into the land of Canaan. It was the Lord's command. A difficult road, and endless. Fatigue and disappointment fostered disbelief.

With his deep knowledge of the human soul, Moses looked for a way to invigorate their faith. He climbed to the highest point on Mount Sinai so as to draw near Heaven. And I AM delivered to him the Ten Commandments.

And God spoke all these words . . .
And all the people saw the
thunder and lightnings,
and the noise of the trumpet,
and the mountain smoking,
and when the people saw it,
they went and stood far off. (Exodus 20.1,18)

Then Moses carved the Ten Commandments on tablets. That was the Law, a moral contract, and the first unshakable article was belief in only one God. The tablets were placed in the Ark, a chest held sacred by Israel.

During hours of rest, Moses would solve differences among people. Helpful instructions would be added to the Law:

Do not deal unjustly with a widow or orphan. If you loan money to the poor, charge no interest.

Worship was to be organized. They were to choose their priests from the tribe of Levi, that is, from the Levites, and these would care for the Holy of Holies.

And the march continued. The Lord's cloud covered and protected the Ark.

At last, the end of the road. Moses faced Canaan, but he was to die before he entered that land. He had appointed Joshua, son of Nun, as his successor, and Joshua would continue his work.

And the Lord said to Moses,
this is the land which I swore unto Abraham,
unto Isaac, and unto Jacob . . .
And I have caused thee to see it with thine eyes,
but thou shalt not go over thither,
and Moses died there . . .
and no man knoweth his sepulchre unto this day . . .
And there arose since
not a prophet in Israel like unto Moses
whom the Lord knew face to face.
(Deuteronomy 34.4,5,6,10)

*

* *

The Land of Promise was beautiful. Samaria with its fertile plains, the gentle Judaea of Jesus with its cypresses. It belonged to no neighboring empire. It was inhabited by various peoples, Bedouins, Canaanites, Philistines who believed in Baal and Astarte.

The twelve tribes of Israel scattered after the death of Joshua. Without a leader, under influences of many kinds, they often intermarried with attractive women of other races, but they preserved their faith.

The Lord was their only guardian. He governed with His angels. He imposed His justice. Lack of faith was the major crime. The unbeliever might follow lawless paths, but there would always be repentance, the appeal out of the depths. And then help — His help.

No one knows where the myth ends and history begins.

History is the action. But the myth, in its mythical dimension, is the suffering soul of the people, its moan. It is the symbol which nourished the people's imagination, and our own.

The years of the Judges help us to understand how fully God-governed was that first epoch.

Many Jews violated the testament and worshipped Baal. Then God became angry and gave great strength to Jabin, King of Canaan. His general, Sisera, had acquired weapons and chariots of war. He cut off every escape and pillaged the lands of the Jews. The country was laid waste. Hopeless, the people of Israel sought refuge in their God. The Lord heard their prayers and took pity on them. He sent a message to their prophetess, Deborah.

In the midst of this chaos, this redeeming picture is wonderful to contemplate. Deborah, with her unshakable faith, sits under a palm tree on Mount Ephraim. Around her all is friction, war, the harsh struggle for survival. She is clear-sighted, wise, inspired by God, respected throughout the land.

She summoned Barak, leader of a neighboring tribe, and gave him this message:

"You will gather together some brave men, and prepare an attack against Sisera."

"I have no chariots. I have no cavalry. I have no such weapons as the enemy," said Barak. "I shall make the attack only if you come with me."

"I shall come," answered Deborah. "But because your faith is little, your triumph will not be complete. A woman will kill Sisera — not you."

Led by the spirit of God, Deborah chose the time of the attack. It was a rainy day. The heavens opened, and torrents swept away the enemy chariots and riders. The horses foundered. Barak on the one hand and the tribe of Ephraim on the other pursued the Canaanites.

Sisera, alone, on foot, lost, took to the mountains. Exhausted, he took refuge in the tent of a nomad woman, Jael, and there he fell asleep. Jael recognized him and killed him as he slept.

What shame for the warrior to be killed by a woman!

Sisera's mother waited for her son. He was always victorious.

"Why are the battle-chariots so late in returning?"

And she rushed from her house in despair, wailing a dirge for her son.

No longer shall we see him dividing the spoils. (Judges 5.30)

But Israel praised the Lord:

Let them that love Him
be like the sun
when He goeth forth in His might (Judges 5.31)

And the land had peace for forty years.

And again.
Temptations on all sides.

The sons of Israel did evil
in the sight of the Lord,
and the Lord delivered them
into the hands of Midian
for seven years. (Judges 6.1)

After seven years of devestation, the Angel of the Lord appeared to Gideon, son of Iona.

Surely I will be with you,
and you will smite the Midianites
as one man. (Judges 6.16)

How did the simple farmer, with only his faith in God, become a warrior, gathering men together to attack the Bedouins?

And the miracle always goes on.

*

* *

There are many such happenings. When we were children we were instructed in religious history. Samson and Delilah, David and Goliath. We listened to them as fairy tales, but they were symbols and sources of inspiration for Christian civilization.

There is Samson's last cry to his God — blind, fettered, with bloody eyes. The cry of one wounded to the depths of his soul.

The precious secret of his superhuman strength was his hair. But dizzy with love in Delilah's embrace, he gave the secret away. Universal symbol of feminine treachery, she lulled him to sleep, cut off his hair, and delivered him, helpless, to the Philistines, who hated him because they were so afraid of him.

How degraded this Hercules of the Bible, this

giant who had been able to break chains as if they were threads! They gouged out his eyes, they beat him, they made fun of him. On a great festival when the satraps of enemy tribes were sacrificing to their god, Dagon, they gathered into their building three thousand men and women to be amused at the spectacle of the enfeebled Samson. Then from utmost desperation, from the bottom of his soul, he prayed:

Lord, Lord, remember me
and give me strength
just one more time! (Judges 16.28)

His hair had begun to grow again, and with it his vigor. With his gigantic hands, he seized the two middle columns that supported the roof and shook them, saying

Let me die with the Philistines. (Judges 6.30)

The columns fell, and the thousands perished with him.

*
* *

The last of the Judges was Samuel.

Samuel, of deep faith and high morality, was the clear link between the world that was passing and the world that was to come. His authority derived from all people. It was for him to judge the leaders who would then rule.

Anna, his mother, had promised him to God, the giver of life and death.

When Samuel reached the age required by the Law, she led him to the temple, and gave him into the care of the priest, Eli. Year by year the boy grew, serving the Lord and His righteousness with a pure heart.

The Lord had singled out Samuel, granting him holiness and the gift of prophecy.

And Samuel grew,
and the Lord was with him,
and let none of his words fall to the ground . . .
And all Israel knew that Samuel was established
to be a prophet of the Lord. (1 Samuel 3.19,20)

Against the terrible Philistines, the other enemy tribes were powerless — Canaanites, Bedouins. The Philistines were always advancing. They had begun to dominate the high places. The Jews decided to give battle. In despair, and to insure victory, they took the Ark with them. But they were defeated, and, worst of all, the Philistines took possession of the Ark.

Desolation concealed the heavens.

The disaster became known. Wailing and lamentations were heard on all sides. Eli, the priest, fell dead. Then the young Samuel revived their lost courage and reorganized the army. They attacked the Philistines and recovered the Ark.

Israel breathed again. The twelve tribes grouped around Samuel. They wanted him for their king. And something deeper. They knew that they must be united. Only a commander accepted by all could lead them victoriously in battle, could confront the enemies surrounding them.

But Samuel belonged entirely to the theocratic era. His relation to God was genuine, direct. He mistrusted the temptations of worldly power.

Now Jehovah Himself sent a message to Samuel:

Hearken unto the voice of the people
. . . and show them the manner of the king
that shall rule over them. (1 Samuel 8.7,9)

Then Samuel searched high and low, and recognized that Saul was God's chosen one. He would make Saul king.

And Samuel said unto Saul . . .
'Stand there a while
that I may make known to thee
the word of God.' (1 Samuel 9.27)

. . . And to the people he said,
'See ye him whom the Lord hath chosen.'
(1 Samuel 10.24)

The twelve tribes met together and proclaimed Saul king.

Thus, with the will of God and the will of the people, the kingdom was established in Israel. This was about the year 1040.

*

*　　*

Saul was a tall, robust man from Geba, a land which had a deep sense of nationality.

He was a brave and tragic spirit, with a divided personality, not at peace with himself. He was suspicious, and did not easily trust others. And the anguish of his mistrust, the madness of his sense of persecution, reached its climax when he was confronted with David.

In the midst of much suffering, the Lord provided an oasis of the highest quality of belief and poetry. This was David. So distant in time, but so close to us through the Psalms and the eternal values he expressed in them.

The youngest of Jesse's sons tended his father's sheep and sang hymns to the accompaniment of his lyre.

But his destiny was something else.

Saul did not bring about a just reign. He did not follow God's way. Off in his village, the aged Samuel grieved over Saul's infidelity. Then again came the word of the Lord.

'How long wilt thou mourn for Saul . . .
fill thy horn with oil,
and I will send thee to Jesse of Bethlehem,
for I have provided me with a king
from among his sons.' (1 Samuel 16.1)

Samuel set out.

At Bethlehem the elders of the city received him.

'I have come to offer sacrifice
to the Lord,' he said.
'Sanctify yourselves and
come with me to the sacrifice.' (1 Samuel 16.5)

He did not wish to reveal his plan. Saul might retaliate. So he sought out Jesse and asked to see his sons. But on no one of them did he see God's sign.

And Samuel said to Jesse,
'Are all your children here?'
And he said,
'There remains yet the youngest,
but behold, he is keeping the sheep.'
And Samuel said to Jesse,
'Send and fetch him,
for we will not sit down
until he comes here.' (1 Samuel 16.11)

And Samuel saw a handsome lad, well set-up, strong, as Michelangelo formed him; blonde and lithe, as Verrocchio painted him: a miracle of grace and charm. Two big, honest eyes gazed at Samuel with courage and trust. This was David.

And he was ruddy,
and withal of a beautiful countenance,
and goodly to look to . . . (1 Samuel 16.12)

And how many secret virtues!

But the Lord said unto Samuel,
'Look not on his countenance,
nor on the height of his stature,
for the Lord seeth not as man seeth;
man looketh on the outward appearance,
but the Lord looketh on the heart.'
(1 Samuel 16.7)

In great secrecy Samuel anointed the young shepherd as King.

He had recognized the Chosen One.

The Lord decided. Time obeyed.

Saul's anxiety was comforted by music. When he learned that David played the lyre melodiously, he called him to stay nearby.

Then something happened, incredible, of great significance. Michelangelo has painted the episode in the Sistine Chapel.

One of the leaders of the Philistines was Goliath, a giant, with a great iron shield, and day after day he threatened Israel. The young shepherd asked Saul for permission to confront him. Some laughed, others pitied the poor lad, but all considered him lost. David took with him only his sling-shot, no other weapon, no shield. But before the enemy attacked, he took aim at Goliath's head, and let fly a stone. The giant fell, and David rushed forward to cut off his head with his own sword.

He returned to the King victorious.

Shouts of joy. Girls at doors and windows sang his praises.

Saul has slain his thousands,
and David his ten thousands. (Samuel 18.7)

But now curious feelings began to trouble Saul's dark soul. Perhaps he marveled at David? Perhaps he hated him? Perhaps he was afraid of him? No one could know. He sent David on the most difficult missions. He promised David his first-born daughter, and then at the last moment changed his mind. He wanted to reduce David in the public eye, to humiliate him.

Jonathan, Saul's son, was always there, and he and David were like brothers. It was he who told David of the danger if he remained near Saul, and it was with Jonathan's help that he went away.

Now David became a wanderer in the desert, hunted, thirsty. But always he trusted in the Lord. When he lay down at night, when he rose at dawn, whether he was in tears, or in fruitful acceptance of his loneliness.

How did this hopeless young shepherd on the mountains of Judaea produce these overflowing fountains of eternal poetry?

Keep me as the apple of thine eye,
Hide me under the shadow of thy wings.
(Psalms 17.8)

Lead me, O Lord, in thy righteousness.
Make thy way straight before my face.
There is no faithfulness in my enemies;
Their throat is an open sepulchre.
They flatter me with their tongues. (Psalms 5.8,9)

Hardhearted sons of men,
Why do you love vanity and seek falsehood?

Saul pursued David like a madman. He gave an impious order that the eighty-five Levites of Nob should be killed because they had covered David's escape.

He chased David to the banks of the Dead Sea. At one moment he was very close to his prey, but exhausted, he fell asleep. David found him so, but did him no evil. He only cut off the edge of his mantle, respecting God's anointed, respecting the sleeping opponent.

Then came a tragic moment. In a fierce battle, the Philistines conquered Israel's army. The hills were covered with the slain. The invincible Saul and his sons, first of them the brave Jonathan, were all dead.

David mourned the lost, mourned his friend.

I am distressed for thee,
my brother Jonathan;
very pleasant hast thou been unto me;
thy love was wonderful,
passing the love of woman. (2 Samuel 1.26)

Saul's presumptive heirs killed each other off. At Hebron, the capital at that time, the twelve tribes met and recognized in David the Lord's anointed. He was now King of Israel.

*

* *

Now came the moment for the Lord to complete the fulfilment of His will — to deliver to His united people the land of Canaan. And among them all, it was David whom He trusted for this work, whom the ages had so long awaited.

David, statesman and soldier, wanted to provide his kingdom with a stable and impregnable capital.

He dreamed Jerusalem worthy of this historic destiny. Its position, in the heart of Palestine, at a central crossroads, built on three hills, offered a natural defense against any enemy. The hill of Zion provided its most formidable fortress. It was occupied by the Canaanites. David ordered it besieged, and promised great honor to the general who would be first to penetrate it. The wily Joab found the way by following an old aqueduct.

Jerusalem became the capital.

David made it beautiful. He brought wise architects from Phoenicia and specialized craftsmen. He brought wood and other materials. Palaces and bastions sprang up. Good general that he was, he hunted down the Philistines and freed the ports.

The unity of the kingdom was achieved.

Now came the moment to fulfill his obligation to the Lord by a civil act of great significance: to bring the Ark to the capital and give it a permanent home. There was an official ceremony. All the Levites participated. And when the procession reached the Gate, the King himself received it with brilliant ritual.

Kingship and worship became identified with each other.

David organized the state and the army. He created a guard made up of devoted mercenaries. The King himself fought in the battles with the brave Joab beside him.

And always he was grateful to the Lord and sang His praise.

Lord, what is man
that Thou art mindful of him?
And the son of man,
that Thou visitest him?
Thou hast made him
a little lower than the angels,
And hast crowned him
with glory and honor.
Thou madest him to have dominion over
the works of Thy hands.
Thou hast put all things under his feet.
(Psalms 8.4-6)

. . . .

He sent from above,
He took me,
He drew me out of many waters.
He delivered me from my strong enemy,
And from them which hated me,

For they were too strong for me.
They prevented
me in the day of my calamity.
But the Lord was my stay.
He brought me forth also into a large place,
He delivered me because He delighted in me.
The Lord rewarded me
according to my righteousness;
According to the cleanness of my hands
He recompensed me.
For I have kept the ways of the Lord,
and have not wickedly departed from my God.
For all his ordinances were before me,
And I did not put away his statutes from me.
(Psalms 18.16-22)

But life itself presented an unlikely ambush.

One night on the palace terrace, sleepless from anxiety, he was disturbed by the lapping of the waves on the shore of the lake. And there in the moonlight he saw a woman bathing. The rays cast a silver light on her shapely body, and played with the harmony of her movement.

"Who can she be?" asked the King, enthralled.

She was Bathsheba, daughter of his warrior, Eliam, and wife of Uriah, the Hittite. David longed to possess her, and called her to his side.

Bathsheba became pregnant. In great perplexity, David summoned his trusted general, Joab.

"Put Uriah in the front line of the hardest fighting," he said.

Uriah was killed.

What David had done displeased the Lord, and He sent the prophet Nathan to speak with the King. And Nathan said: "There was a rich man with flocks and herds and goods. There was also a poor man who had only one ewe-lamb which he loved and cherished. And the rich man took the ewe-lamb away from the poor man."

"That man must be severely punished," the King ordered.

"But you are that man," said the prophet. "It is you who must be punished. You took the wife of Uriah the Hittite, and you left him to be killed in the battle with the Ammonites."

David cried out in despair, "My God, I have sinned."

He humbled himself and passionately sought forgiveness.

O Lord, do not condemn me in Thy anger,
Do not punish me in Thy fury.
Be merciful to me, O Lord,
for I am weak.
Come back, O Lord, and set my soul free.
Deliver me in Thy mercy.
I am wearied with groaning. (Psalms 6.1,2,4,6)

The punishment did not lessen. Bathsheba's child became ill. David fasted and prayed that the baby should recover. He was not heard, and the little one did not live.

Other disasters followed. Intrigues within his own family. Dissension and hate among his children.

His first-born son, Ammon, fell in love with his beautiful half-sister, Tamar, and lay with her. In despair, Tamar took refuge with her full-brother, Absalom. He killed Ammon and fled. Eventually he reached Hebron, raised an army, revolted against his father, and conquered Jerusalem.

The aging King took refuge in the desert. The mercenaries of the Philistines and the old leaders remained faithful to him.

His hope in God did not diminish.

Lord, how are they increased that trouble me!
Many are they that rise up against me!
Many are they which say of my soul
There is no help for him in God.
But Thou, O Lord, art a shield for me,
My glory, and the lifter-up of my head.
I cried unto the Lord with my voice,
And he heard me out of His holy hill.
(Psalms 3.1-4)

Absalom finally lost the battle and in his hasty flight, his thick hair was caught in the branch of a tree, and he was hanged. His horse continued to run without a rider. Joab killed him.

What a painful victory for the King! He loved Absalom and his violent death was a heavy blow. In despair he returned to Jerusalem.

Now he was weak, and dispirited. His children searched Israel for a young virgin to care for him and warm his old body. Abishag was found to be the best, full of grace and charm and innocence.

It is possible that Abishag of Shunem was the inspiration of the Song of Songs.

> *And the damsel was very fair, and she cherished the King, and ministered to him, but the King knew her not.* (1 Kings 1.4)

His final concern was the unity of the kingdom.

As his heir, David favored Solomon, his son by Bathsheba. The prophet Nathan and the Levites also preferred him. David asked the prophet Nathan and the priest Sadok to support Solomon as King of Israel.

> *Mount my son Solomon on my mule and escort him down to Gibon, and there the priest Zadok and the prophet Nathan shall anoint him King over Israel, and sound the trumpet and shout 'Long live King Solomon.'* (1 Kings 1.33-34)

David sensed that his end was near. He called Solomon and spoke prophetically:

> *I am going the way of all the earth.*
> *Be strong, and show yourself a man.*
> (1 Kings 2.1-2)

They buried him on the hill of Jerusalem where the Ark was kept. What does this mean? Truly he was "going the way of all the earth."

I have spent more time over David because, like Moses, he is a great peak.

Chosen of God, he built the state of Israel.

He was neither prophet nor mystic. But he believed in the Lord God, and worshipped Him passionately. With an unrivalled moral sense, he surmounted all the burdens and weaknesses of his difficult life.

David suffered in his solitude, suffered in his sin, but he was always great, and out of the depths he would call on God. His thinking, both the idea and its expression, builds a bridge to Heaven.

The Lord trieth the righteous:
But the wicked and him that loveth violence
His soul hateth.
For the righteous Lord loves righteous deeds,
And the upright shall behold His face.
(Psalms 11.5,7)

And for the weak, he would write in humility:

O Lord, Thou wilt hear the desire of the meek;
Thou wilt strengthen their heart,
Thou wilt incline Thine ear to do justice
To the fatherless and oppressed,
So that man who is of the earth
May strike terror no more. (Psalms 10.17-18)

And what a marvel! — a thousand years before the birth of Christ, from a primitive people, a poet was born whose sublimity even today we can only try to approach!

What does time matter? The spirit waits. And after selfish desires and wars, we hear softly and simply, a distant melody of hope, the footsteps of Christ the Lord coming down to earth!

*
*   *

Now came Solomon, the mythical King of Israel, the King of riches and luxury. A wise statesman, he appointed magistrates and brought order into his rule.

As a diplomat, he tried to avoid wars, to establish good relations with neighboring states.

Among his many wives were daughters of neighboring kings, those of Egypt and of Tyre.

At the same time, he was developing his army with chariots and cavalry.

From his father, he inherited harbors, and so he acquired ships. Thus he developed commerce. His father-in-law, Hiram, King of Tyre, ruled the sea, and he taught Israel the art of navigation.

Jerusalem grew rich. Word of its royal power was heard even in far-off Arabia. And the Queen of Sheba, with a rich entourage, arrived in Jerusalem to visit its royalty.

It pleases the Jews to remember his kingship, a kingship of peace and wealth.

They will attribute to him all the virtues — wisdom, righteousness, great poetical works.

We are certain of no facts. The wonderful Song of Songs was not written down until three centuries later. It may be a translation. But Solomon's great work, which dazzled and lived and still lives, is the Temple.

On a hill of Zion, perhaps at the spot where Abraham would have sacrificed Isaac, Solomon erected the Temple. He insisted on the finest materials, the most skilled craftsmen.

He made an agreement with the King of Tyre. Hiram was to give gold and cedar, and special workmen, in exchange for oil, wine, and grain offered by Israel.

For seven years they labored tirelessly —architects, builders, artisans. At last the Temple emerged — magnificent, imposing, worthy to house the Ark.

Solomon offered the first prayer:

Lord God of Israel,
One God in heaven
and on earth.

The legendary temple of Solomon, whether in the fullness of its glory or in ruins, remains for this historic people the chief symbol of worship. On the part of its wall that still stands, among its fissures, Jews of today place written appeals to the Lord.

Great wealth carries within itself the seeds of dissolution. It creates classes, the proud and the humble. It creates factions.

But the God of Israel desired justice and moderation. What had become of Samuel's austere administration? and even David's? Under Solomon the great power was money. The spiritual purity of the race was threatened.

And there was also now the temptation to idolatry. The King's foreign wives introduced their idols. The Egyptian wife arrived with a band of shamans and demanded altars for her own gods. For political reasons, Solomon acceded to her desires. And in the holy city they show the Mount of Skandalon where altars to idols were once erected. Belief in one God, the very foundation of the kingdom, was tottering.

Solomon was succeeded by Rehoboham, his son by a foreign wife. He was intoxicated by power, and became harsh and violent.

Israel rose in rebellion against Judaea, recognizing the kingship of Jeroboam.

War between the two states lasted for fifty years, and exhausted both of them.

In the kingdom of the North, there were queens of other religions, wasteful women of lax morality, and they imposed the worship of Baal and Astarte.

However, in this disorganization of the royal work, in the tragic decline of popular morale, the seed did not die. Rather it gave birth to the most significant period of the Bible, the Prophecy.

Renan was to say about this: "The religious future of Israel was immediately dependent on the freedom of prophecy, and this freedom could not co-exist with a strong state."

*

*　　*

What purity, what savagery, not described elsewhere in the Bible, pour forth from the books of

Prophecy!

They are tragic figures, the Prophets, living in solitude, but carrying within them the darkness where the Logos is engendered: the Logos conceived in obscurity, and emerging as the Absolute. An other-wordly creation lighted the burning heart of God, and was transferred to the spirit of the prophets.

From earliest times in Israel we meet men of the purest spirit and unshakable faith, dedicated to the Lord. They knew God's will for the future. The Jews respected them and listened to them, as did Deborah and Samuel and Nathan. Now personalities of the first order were fearlessly opposing the forces of evil.

They are called the Writer Prophets because they have left written testimony in the Bible. There are four major ones: Isaiah whose genius is recognized throughout the world; Jeremiah; Ezekiel; and Daniel. There are the twelve minor prophets as well.

Dressed in skins of animals, they lived lives of utmost frugality. This was necessary if they were to be free in their judgments of the social depravity of the time.

They disdained the fawning courtiers, the hypocrites. They were ashamed to possess slaves. They condemned the hangmen.

They were governed by the passion for the Absolute.

Prophecy in the Old Testament is a powerful force. It reveals irregularities; it predicts punishment; it is the voice of the angered God.

Their first phrase is always: "Thus says the Lord . . . " And their style has unfailing impact. They do not limit themselves to writing. They are men of action. Their phrases, dictated by a force outside themselves, can move worlds.

This is Isaiah's prayer:

My soul yearns for Thee in the night,
my spirit within me earnestly seeks Thee.
(Isaiah 26.9)

In despair at the disasters he is obliged to prophecy, Jeremiah calls on God. He wants to say no more. But God's words burn within him.

If I say, "I will not mention Him,
or speak any more in His name,
There is in my heart as it were
a burning fire shut up in my bones,
And I am weary with holding it in,
and I cannot. (Jeremiah 20.9)

Then he relents, controls himself, and asks to repent. God shows compassion toward him.

"I am forgiving," says the Lord,
And I do not keep my anger forever."
(Micah 7.18)

The prophet Amos, he too speaks for righteousness:

I hate, I despise your feasts and
I take no delight in your solemn assemblies . . .
But let justice roll down like waters,
and righteousness like an overflowing stream.
(Amos 5.21,24)

Ezekiel is fierce-looking and lives in a cave. But a hope lights up his prophecy.

We are still in the East. The present works for the future. Let us hope and believe that.

What Isaiah tore down, Ezekiel builds up again. In the midst of oppression, we glimpse freedom.

He will say:

You will have neither kings nor magistrates.
You will be one people,
and you will believe in One God.

And the poetry of God's despair! God will give a new spirit, a new heart to mankind. Till now it was of stone. Time now to put in its place a heart of flesh.

Thus saith the Lord . . . ! "I will cleanse you.
I will cleanse you.
I will give a new spirit within you.
I will take the heart of stone from your body,
and give you a heart of flesh.
I will put my spirit into you." (Ezekiel 25-27)

And Ezekiel ends with the great message, the message of the coming of Christ:

Then he brought me back to the outer gate of the sanctuary, which faces east; and it was shut. And he said to me, "This gate shall remain shut; it shall not be opened, and no one shall enter by it; for the Lord, the God of Israel, has entered by it; therefore it shall remain shut. Only the Prince may sit within to eat bread before the Lord." (Ezekiel 44.1-3)

It is the prophets who magnanimously give man his moral sense.

Then it was for Jesus to build the world on the unshakeable foundations of love.

It was for Christ God, in accordance with Ezekiel's prophecy, to come and share His bread with the Lord, to make us members of the kingdom of the Spirit.

The Lord shall come in

The Lord Shall Come In

The moment has come for the Closed Gate to be opened. The moment has come when I must be humble and ready. Perhaps after my concentration among His roots, I may be worthy to hear His footsteps.

11 March 1984

We set out for Israel. We were a large company, Greeks and Jews, all colleagues in the effort to carry out a great plan, with a common culture and a common memory.

I felt grateful to all these people. Each was making some contribution to this journey.

Our first day's stop was at Tel-Aviv. We visited the Museum of the Diaspora. Brilliantly assembled, it presents a lively historical retrospective of the Hebrew race through time.

Countless Judaic symbols from the various European countries, and many representations in miniature of the synagogue. The most elaborate was the synagogue of Amsterdam with 336 symbolic candles.

From Tel-Aviv our excursion to the ancient city of Jaffa was very interesting. This is the old port, used by Solomon for the import of gold and ivory and fragrant wood. Boats with workmen came there from Phoenicia.

Historic old buildings, picturesque settlements. Little bays where the Mediterranean slips in with its blue charm.

That evening there was an official dinner with exchange of greetings, offered by the President of the Graeco-Judaic Society.

At ten o'clock, free again, we set out for the Holy City.

The road to Jerusalem ascends. The night was luminous and seemed to take all mankind into its embrace. As always, I sat beside the driver, but, longing to live those moments to the fullest, I managed an inner solitude.

It was about midnight when we reached Jerusalem.

The night before Monday. Something was missing, and something was present. I stood by the open window, all but disembodied, entering into the mystery. I was seeking to draw near a Presence that I did not see, but a Presence that was there. I stepped back into the room. I wanted to go out into the streets, into the darkness, alone. Perhaps without actually seeing Him, I would feel His presence, wrapped in His holy silence, walking beside me.

This was the boundary of Heaven, His own earth. Every inch bore His footprints.

I was wakened by the daylight. Through the

shutters, the room became aglow. I opened the window.

Unbelievable. The sun had risen, and made the stone more golden, wherever it was to be found — in churches, in walls, in fortresses, at every corner. I was so dazzled that I could scarcely tell whether the stone gilded the sun, or the sun the stone.

Jerusalem! Land of His Passion!

I took a deep breath. The same breeze would have been cooling the atmosphere at that dawn. The same light would have made the city golden on that day.

Today is our real time. His time.

I went early into the streets, looking for Him at every corner. A sudden drop of rain struck my face and startled me. The rug with little flowers spread under my feet was for Him. I felt the mystery in the air.

Gethsemane, the heart's deepest anguish. The olive trees. Long since, they had had certain dimension in my imagination. Now, unexpectedly, they were even more distorted, more tormented.

I sat down on a low wall. Tranquillity, silence. Within their foliage, His secret spirit. In front of me, the two-thousand-year-old olive tree, wisest of all.

Had it perhaps seen Him?

It must have heard His sigh.

My soul is sorrowful unto death. (Matthew 26.38)

And it spread its arms to contain His pain. The pain of the great decision. Its thousand eyes opened in wonder and belief.

I heard the dripping of His sweat.
Drops of blood falling on the earth. (Luke 22.44)

I fell on my knees and gently touched the soil. My heart was pounding.

At the Holy Sepulchre, among the many pilgrims, there He was.
Alone at the foot of His cross, I heard His words as their echo struck the walls of the Temple.

Father, forgive them for they know not what they do. (Luke 23.34)

Christ, my God, how did You endure Your nails?
And for a moment, I seemed to see those nails, blazing suns, lighting up the universe.

Here is the first day of Creation.
Until now — preparation.
And the Lord said:
Let Christ be born Man, and Christ was born.

And the Man leaned toward the beasts, and the beasts were tamed. Others linger in the darkness, and in time will be tamed by His Logos.

Thy light a daily revelation,
in Thy struggle to open the hearts of men —
Thy spirit the substance of life.

At the wall remaining from Solomon's Temple, wailing and petitions to God. Many people there.

I have tried in vain to imagine the place where Jesus might have stood.

*

*   *

Each one of us has two selves. The one self acts, fulfills daily duties, participates in the problems of our time. The other, the innermost self, hears within a secret melody, a clear command to love. And if we merit the Grace, a Presence follows.

The Patriach of Jerusalem, Diodoros, is a lively, active man and, with the other bishops, he welcomed us at the Patriarchate. There was serious dialogue about the problems of Orthodoxy.

Later at his residence on the Mount of Olives, guests gathered for dinner. They were our traveling companions, Greeks and Jews. Speeches, conferral of decorations, exchange of gifts, discussions.

I ventured various questions about the Kibbutz Qiryat Anavim where we had visited that afternoon, but connected dialogue was difficult. We were too many.

On Tuesday we were taken to the Memorial of the Holocaust (Yad Vachem). In memory of the martyrs and heroes. A vast area with impressive monuments, and rows of trees marked with names of friends. Inside the Museum, millions of the dead came alive in their pictures, bodies without flesh, faces whose only expression was acceptance, humility.

Images of horror, portrayals of Hell. Naked women ready for the furnace. Children with fear and dread in their eyes at the unexplainable surroundings. But how is it possible to explain that in the civilized twentieth century a wild sadism and science worked together for years to dishonor, to persecute, and aimlessly to kill millions of human beings?

> *A nation meted out . . . a nation*
> *hopeless and trodden down.* (Isaiah 18.2)

Reuben Daphni, former ambassador, was our guide at the Museum, and one could hear the depth of bitterness in his voice.

Where could we find support for the renewal of our belief in the human race? At this point in our visit, it was a gift to take us immediately to the Hadassah Medical Center to see Chagall's stained glass, shining shapes and colors that created fascinating compositions. Redemptive art — a way at last for man to face his Creator with dignity.

Rain and cold. I was frozen. They were waiting for us at the National Hebrew Library of the University. Some of the books belong to the sixteenth century. There are Greek books written in Hebrew letters. One of these was written in Greek by a Greek iconographer of the era. I copied a few lines. Both the language and the recipe interested me: "A little ochre, a little glue, a little egg yolk, as much as you like, to make it golden. After all these, add the red for the tops of the flowers, gild it with raki, and it will be wonderful."

At noon, Teddy Kollek, mayor of Jerusalem, was expecting us. He is a cultivated Viennese, beloved by the people. The atmosphere was easy, pleasant. Patriarch Diodoros was also a guest. In deference to him, there was abundant fasting-food. I sat next to him, and was glad for the opportunity to know him better.

I learned that the Patriarchate supports forty-five Greek schools, two gymnasia, and a lyceum at Bethlehem. It is active at all levels.

At the Museum we were eager to see the new scrolls in the Shrine of the Book. They were discovered in stone jars found in caves near the Dead Sea.

In order to house them properly, they have built an underground museum with cave-like passages. Scientific diligence is everywhere evident — in the heating, the lighting, the safety construction of the building. They have foreseen the danger of bombardment, earthquake, fire, and theft.

March 14. The day designated by the University for the official inauguration of the Greek wing.

At nine in the morning, before the ceremony, we were received by Mr. Chaim Herzog, President of Israel. All was carefully programmed, and there was plenty of time at our disposal.

Our escort was Nati Tamir, Advisor to the Ministry of Foreign Affairs, an open-hearted, cultivated man. He was waiting for us at the entrance.

At the Presidential Palace there was also Barnea, Israel's Acting Ambassador to Greece. The day before in Athens, there had been a plan to assassinate him. The assassin did not know that Barnea was absent in Jerusalem.

President Herzog, from Ireland, was formerly Ambassador to the United States — a good lawyer, well-informed, judicious. His wife is from Alexandria, cordial, intelligent, friendly.

His office was decorated with modern tapestries by the well-known Ardon whose work I had already seen at the Hadassah Medical Center.

At last we went to the Mount Scopus campus of the University. A modern maze, in shining cleanliness. The hall of the Hellenic House was crowded. The Patriarch was there. Speeches were made, in Greek, English, and Hebrew. My husband spoke first after an introduction by the Rector. Then Constantine Trypanis, in his Oxford English, reviewed the common history of the two ancient civilizations.

I wandered off and lost my friends. A man I did not know approached me and said he was to drive us to the Academy for lunch.

"But where are the others?" I asked.

"Wait here, and I will find them," he said, leaving me beside a rather antiquated car.

Presently he returned with my husband and Trypanis.

We set off. I sat beside him. This man whom I assumed to be a chauffeur gave evidence of being a wise man. His speech was cultivated, and he could speak about everything. I asked where he had studied and he referred to two universities.

All was in readiness at the home of E. E. Urbach, President of the Academy and a likely candidate for the President of the State. A table was reserved for the Academicians, and one seat was unoccupied — until filled by our driver, he too an academician.

Israel's socialism is genuine, a natural brotherhood. You work with your hands or you work with your mind. The Israelis love and respect the educated as they love and respect the brave and the poor.

I said to Nati:

"At last it's time for Bethlehem. We have no more appointments. Today is the great day."

"Let's go," said Nati, with respect for my personal feelings.

So off we went. Again I sat with our regular driver, Jacob, so as to have the best view of what we would see on the way.

Simple houses, well-designed buildings . . . Rebecca's well. Jacob was alwas obliging, ready to explain the most important sites. I didn't listen carefully. I was thinking of the Holy Mother.

How close She is to us throughout our lives!

In his first poem when he was alone abroad, George Seferis wrote:

Let my impoverished soul
expire at Thy holy feet,
divine, compassionate One,
while I kneel with my head
on my mother's knee.

And when our mother died, "Look!" said our brother, Angelos, pointing to the silver Virgin hanging above her pillow.

Two tears were rolling down that sweetest of faces. Later I wiped them away. Orphans that we then were, I felt a Mother still near us.

Many years later during the Occupation in 1943, the Germans came, planning to occupy our house in Plaka. How I pleaded with the Virgin! And that afternoon I saw Her, a Presence as in a dream. She spread Her grey veil, and closed Kydathinaion Street to the foreign army as it approached.

Again on the first of May in 1944, I remember Her as She stood in the midst of the clothing cast off by the nameless victims of the executioners. I remember Her among the mothers as they wept and sang their dirges. Now there She stood, as She had stood by the Cross, the Mother of the Crucified One with His pierced side. The sword of the aged Simeon shone brightly.

Mother of the World, ever quick to hear us, Savior of us all.

We reached Bethlehem.

We had to stoop to enter by the side door of the great basilica of the Nativity. I stood still, entranced by the poetic rhythm of its structure. The row of Corinthian columns seemed never to end, and the proportions emerged organically with absolute economy. Their harmony was overwhelming.

Time has respected what Justinian built.

The figures on the walls, and the parts of the floor which have been cleaned, reveal mosaics of the Komneni.

An irregular staircase led down to the Manger. The Star was shining. The Virgin held Her Babe in strong, tender embrace. I heard Her memories, Her inner joy:

Today is my very own hour.
I hold You in my arms, newborn,
Dazzled by Your shining light.
You are still my flesh,

And neither the evil ones,
Nor the Spirit, nor even Your own soul
Can take You from me.
I am Your world.

Is it possible? At this point on earth, this great, this infinite happening! The most gentle of women, the Holy Mother, brought God into the world. How can man's mind contain so vast a concept?

And by God's grace, it has come about that I am here to participate in the mystical joy of this hour. The Manger is flooded with light.

Time, I felt, stood still, the then, the now, the what-is-to-come, all standing subdued, beside Her.

Prophecies and scriptures, psalms and ceremonies, the ultimate of comfort and hope —all there round the Star of the Nativity.

Like the Magi, pilgrims were coming with gifts — in nylon bags, mark of the present. I seemed to hear verses from the Salutations to the Virgin:

Hail, celestial ladder by which God came down!
Hail, dawn of a mystical day . . .

We climbed up again by the same stair, and again I was facing the rhythmic splendor of the Basilica. Faith and art and power have joined to create the masterpiece which shelters Her.

As we returned to Jerusalem in the fading light of the evening, shining clouds traveled with us.

That evening I did not see people. Beside my open window, I lost myself in Jerusalem as it slowly lighted up.

Softly the Holy Night slipped into my room in the King David Hotel.

Thursday – a day to myself.

Clouds gathered. Big drops of rain.

I entered on the narrow road of the Martyrdom. What secret light cast the great shadow I was following?

At the station of Pilate, I opened the gate and stood in the courtyard.

Someone beside me sighed deeply. I turned suddenly.

Whoever is tormented by love looks for a presence.

I went on.

Voices around me, open shops.

But for me the road was deserted – only His footprints.

The storm grew stronger.

Alone, and beaten by the wind, I slowly ascended the road of the Passion.

I knew that You were there, that whatever I longed for, You too were longing for. You wanted me there. Your power, a deep well, was shaking the foundations. That strong north wind was uniting us, helping my own participation.

And now You are drawn to Golgotha.

Your crucified arms open forever in Your wide embrace.

An endless pilgrimage.

I could not see. I was transfixed again at the foot of the Cross, at the point where they had planted Your Cross.

A choked echo, and the broken stones looked at me in heavy sorrow. "The rocks were rent . . . " (Matthew 27.51)

*

*   *

Bishop Daniel of Thavor opened the Treasury for us. He showed us the cross of the Emperor Heraklios with wood from the True Cross, worked with precious stones. There was also the cross of John Palaiologos, smaller, also with a segment from the True Cross. There were gold embroidered tunicles and stoles from many patriarchs.

The Patriarchate is located next to the Church of the Crucifixion. Patriarch Diodoros was expecting us at his residence. There were others present. It is a huge complex — salons, outdoor terraces, courtyards at various levels, structures above and below.

From a veranda I saw, very close by, the Church of Saint John the Baptist, and I remembered that the Empress Athenais was its founder.

There was also the Patriarchal Library with many manuscripts, scrolls, and decrees of the Sultans.

The Museum occupies a new building with modern heating and lighting. All finds from the area have been carefully assembled here. Some of the artifacts are ancient, others from the time of the Crusades; among these, busts of Moses and Aaron, joined. There are also embroidered stoles of enormous value, on one of them the entire Tree of Jesse.

Two of the churches have remarkable old ikons. In the Church of Saint Constantine, there is "The Falling Asleep of Saint Ephraim" and "The Supplication of Saint Constantine and Saint Helen" by Andrea Pavia. Also "Noli Me Tangere," the masterpiece of Emmanuel Lombardos, and "The Holy Apostles" by Daniel the Monk. The Church of Hagia Thekla also has fine old ikons.

Evening now. A low black cloud darkened the window. Whatever was worthy in what we had lived, the light of the sun and of the night, the motion of the tree in the hum of the breeze, the green gold of the fields and the blooming rose, the snow-covered heights of the mountain and the blue of the sea; whatever was worthy in what we had lived, in thought and struggles, in poetry and music, in dreams and aspiration, the whole of life, of worthwhile life, became substance in this crucified embrace.

The Crucifixion spread to all Jerusalem, to the

whole of creation, to the roots of the suffering heart. Drops of blood fell and opened a depth in His Logos beyond understanding.

As the firmament grew dark, as an earthquake shook the city, all suffering was included in the holy order of that most terrible hour.

Suffering beyond measure. The ultimate of love, the ultimate of pain.

The failing mind whispered a sad lullaby, borne from a deep longing, a dirge mystical, erotic.

*

*   *

Next day to the airport.

Somewhere there, between the two cities:

> *that same day two of them were on their way to a village called Emmaus, which lay about seven miles from Jerusalem, and they were talking together about all these happenings. As they talked and discussed with one another, Jesus Himself came up and walked along with them; but something kept their eyes from seeing who it was.* (Luke 24.13-16)

And now it was we who were going to Emmaus. The first rays of the sun lighted up Jesus' road. Then it had been night. It was the Logos which claimed the time, and the time was night.

Today the brilliance of the dawn overwhelmed our soul.

Longing for the Gospel hour, I followed His road.

"Jesus Himself . . . walked with them . . ."

How strong this pull back to His earthly life! What human concern brought Him back to us? On that day, the last rays of the sun shone on His beautiful face, summoning Him to the glory of Heaven. But the humble earth, the suffering earth, held Him, tied Him still to His unending obligation.

The disciples were not looking at Him; they were discussing what lay so heavily on their souls: the great injustice of the time — His passion.

Then He spoke:

"But didn't you know all this had been predicted by the Prophets?"

Then He walked on with them, so simply, so naturally, that today we cannot be sure: perhaps someone we do not recognize, approaching us in the tragic hour of doubt, may bring us something from Jesus.

The unknown one may take the bread — he may bless it, he may divide it. He may perform this sacred act of life, and be lost.

How often since then do You come back, longing to walk again on Your beloved soil? It may be that in the warm dust as it caresses Your bare feet, You will sense something of my shattered soul, which, departing, I leave with You.